T0011681

IN RECITAL®
with All-Time Favorites

ABOUT THE SERIES • A NOTE TO THE TEACHER

In Recital® with All-Time Favorites is a wonderful collection of popular arrangements of children's classroom songs, traditional favorites, and the most popular folk songs ever! This series has something for everyone! Irving Berlin, George M. Cohan, and Stephen Foster are just a few of the outstanding songwriters featured in this series. The excellent arrangers of this series, Nancy Lau, Chris Lobdell, Edwin McLean, Kevin Olson, and Robert Schultz, have created engaging arrangements of some of the best All-Time Favorites, all of which have been carefully leveled to ensure success with this repertoire. We know that to motivate, the teacher must challenge the student with attainable goals. This series makes that possible. You will find favorites that are easy to sing along with as well as recital-style arrangements. This series complements other FJH publications and will help you plan student recital repertoire. The books include CDs with complete performances designed to assist with recital preparation as well as for pure listening pleasure. Throughout this series you will find interesting background information for each piece by Dave and Becky Olsen.

 Use the enclosed CD as a teaching and motivational tool. For a guide to listening to the CD, turn to page 44.

Production: Frank J. Hackinson
Production Coordinators: Joyce Loke and Satish Bhakta
Cover Art Concept: Helen Marlais
Cover Design: Terpstra Design, San Francisco, CA
Cover Illustration: Marcia Donley
Engraving: Tempo Music Press, Inc.
Printer: Tempo Music Press, Inc.

ISBN 1-56939-777-5

ORGANIZATION OF THE SERIES
IN RECITAL® WITH ALL-TIME FAVORITES

The series is carefully leveled into the following six categories: Early Elementary, Elementary, Late Elementary, Early Intermediate, Intermediate, and Late Intermediate. Each of the works has been selected for its artistic as well as its pedagogical merit.

Book Four — Early Intermediate, reinforces the following concepts:

- Students play pieces with common time signatures as well as compound meters.

- Students play pieces with more intricate finger crossovers.

- Students learn to play pieces with changes of tempo and articulations, and use the pedal.

- Major, minor, root position chords, and their inversions are reinforced, as well as subdominant, dominant, and major seventh chords.

- Left-hand parts increase in intricacy with more involved accompanimental figures and *ostinato* patterns. Two voices at the same time are sometimes played in the right hand.

- Hand positions expand larger than a fifth.

- Keys of C major, G major, F major, D major, A minor, and E minor.

The Glow-Worm was arranged as an unequal-part duet. *The Campbells Are Comin'* and *My Old Kentucky Home* were arranged as equal-part duets. The rest of the selections are solos.

TABLE OF CONTENTS

ABOUT THE PIECES AND COMPOSERS

The Rock Island Line

First recorded in the 1930s by Leadbelly (Huddie Ledbetter), *The Rock Island Line* is an American blues/folk song that is supposedly about the "Chicago, Rock Island and Pacific Railroad" which was a Class 1 (freight) railroad. Leadbelly was a versatile blues and folk musician who not only played 12-string guitar, but also played violin, piano, harmonica, and accordion. He claimed that he first heard the song from a prison work gang during his travels, when in fact he was in prison himself for attempted murder. Over the years the song has been recorded by artists such as Johnny Cash, Bobby Darin, and John Lennon.

In the Good Old Summer Time

With music by George Evans and lyrics by Ren Shields, this song was first published in 1902 after several previous unsuccessful attempts. Most publishers felt the song wouldn't remain popular once the summer season had ended, but when the song was included in the musical comedy show *The Defender*, they changed their minds. The song was an instant hit, with the audience joining in to sing the chorus at each performance. *In the Good Old Summer Time* was recorded by John Philip Sousa's band in 1903 and has remained a standard in the years since.

The Yankee Doodle Boy

George M. Cohan wrote *The Yankee Doodle Boy* for the Broadway Musical *Little Johnny Jones* which premiered in 1904. In the play, Yankee Doodle was a horse that was entered in the English Derby. Cohan was fond of including snippets of other popular songs in his works, hence the reference to the original *Yankee Doodle* toward the end of the refrain!

George M. Cohan was sometimes called "The Man Who Owns Broadway," and in 1942 a movie based on his life—*Yankee Doodle Dandy*—was released.

The Campbells Are Comin'

There are a number of ancient pipe tunes connected with the Scottish Clan (Gaelic for a family group) known as the Campbells, but no tune is more associated with them than *The Campbells Are Comin'*. The Gaelic name of the original song is *Baile Ionaraora* (the town of Inveraray), and the words in Gaelic reflect upon the feelings of the piper-composer who apparently was less than pleased with the hospitality and food he was offered as the piper at a local wedding. The words we commonly know today boast of the Clan's march to Loch Leven Castle.

The Glow-Worm

First published in 1902, *The Glow-Worm* was first featured in the musical score of the English musical *The Girl Behind the Counter,* which ran on Broadway between 1907 and 1908. Years later, it was a major hit for the Mills Brothers–a jazz vocal quartet (and actual brothers) popular in the 1940s and 1950s. Their version spent twenty-one weeks on the charts and three weeks at No. 1 during 1952. *The Glow-Worm* has the distinction of being danced to by famed ballerina Anna Pavlova in her *Empire Gavotte,* recorded as a Christmas song (with alternate lyrics) by Mel Tormé, and being played on the saxophone in an episode of *I Love Lucy.*

The House of the Rising Sun

Originally an American ballad, *The House of the Rising Sun* tells the tale of a life gone wrong. The oldest existing recording by singer Tom Ashley (who learned the song from his grandfather) dates back to 1933. The most well-known recording was the 1964 version by The Animals, a British group that rose to fame along with The Beatles during the so-called 'British Invasion' of the mid-1960s.

The Rock Island Line

Traditional
arr. Edwin McLean

want to ride it, you will go like you're a - fly-in'. Buy your tick-et at the sta-tion on the

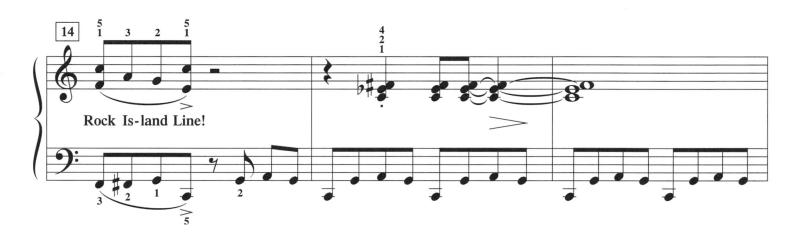

Rock Is-land Line!

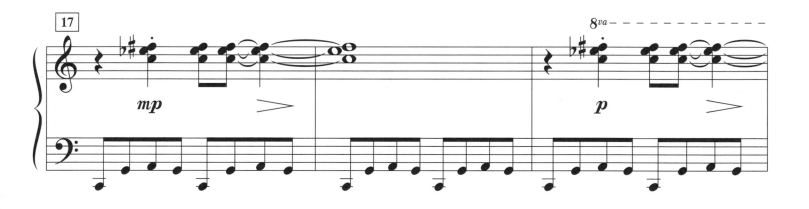

mp   p

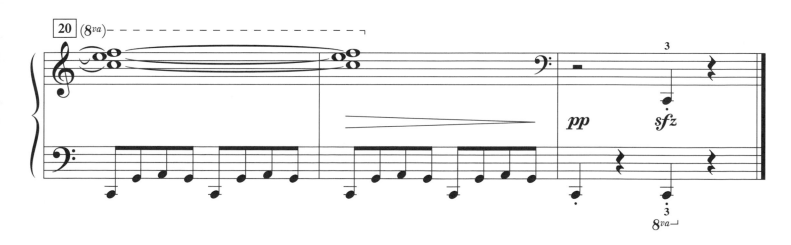

pp   sfz

In the Good Old Summer Time

Music by George Evans
Lyrics by Ren Shields
arr. Kevin Olson

The Yankee Doodle Boy

Music and Lyrics by George M. Cohan
arr. Robert Schultz

The Campbells Are Comin'
Secondo

Traditional Scottish Air
arr. Kevin Olson

The Campbells Are Comin'
Primo

Traditional Scottish Air
arr. Kevin Olson

FJH2044

Secondo

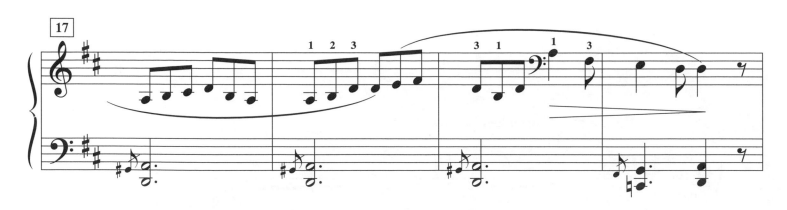

Primo

The Glow-Worm

Music by Paul Lincke
English Lyrics by Lilla Cayley Robinson
arr. Nancy Lau

Teacher Accompaniment: (*Student plays one octave higher*)

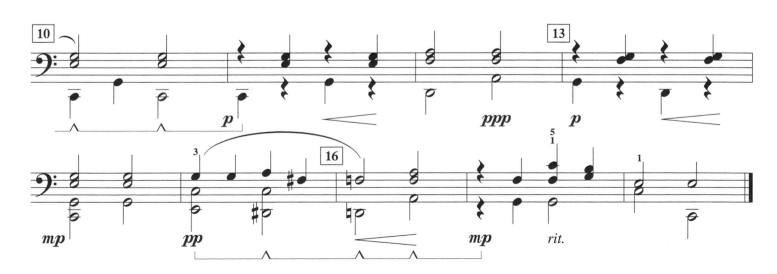

The House of the Rising Sun

Traditional
arr. Robert Schultz

K-K-K-Katy

Music and Lyrics by Geoffrey O'Hara
arr. Robert Schultz

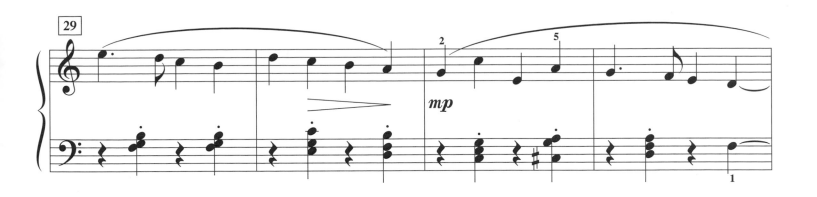

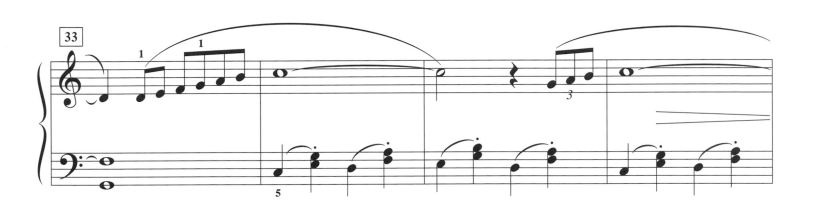

My Old Kentucky Home
Secondo

Music and Lyrics by Stephen C. Foster
arr. Chris Lobdell

My Old Kentucky Home
Primo

Music and Lyrics by Stephen C. Foster
arr. Chris Lobdell

FJH2044

Secondo

Primo

Shine On, Harvest Moon

Music by Nora Bayes-Norworth
Lyrics by Jack Norworth
arr. Nancy Lau

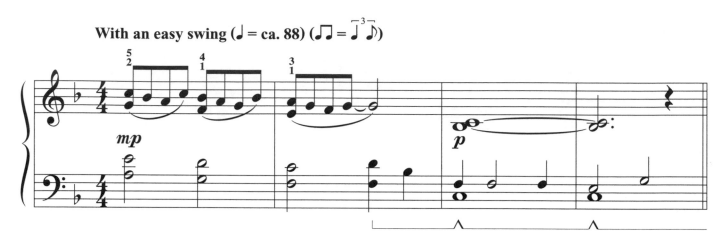

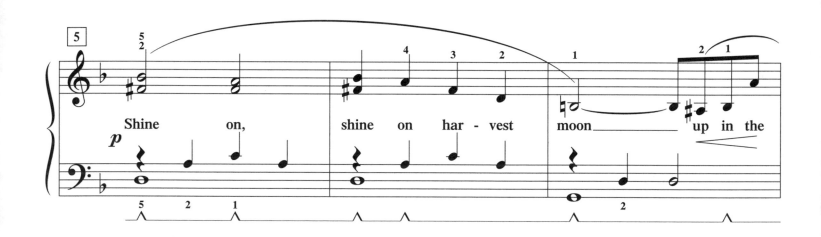

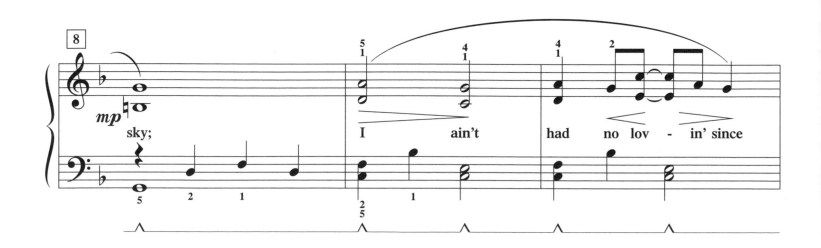

Maple Leaf Rag

Scott Joplin
arr. Edwin McLean

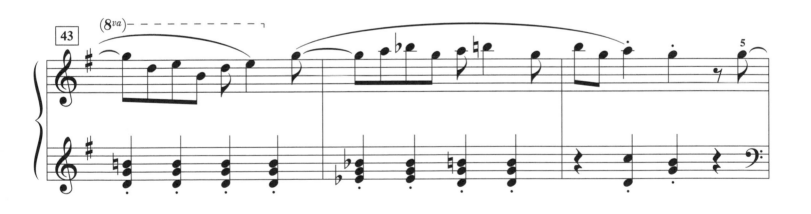

Ragtime Cowboy Joe

Music by Lewis F. Muir and Maurice Abrahams
Lyrics by Grant Clarke
arr. Chris Lobdell

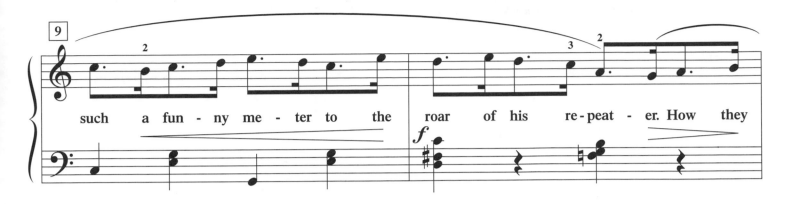

such a fun-ny me-ter to the roar of his re-peat-er. How they

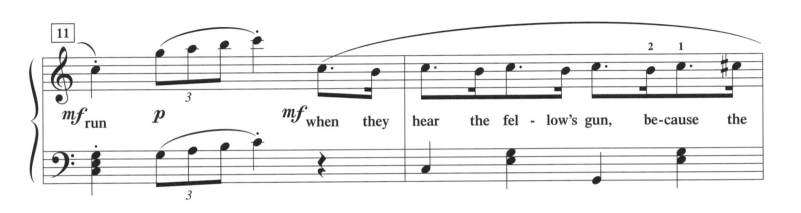

mf run   *p*   *mf* when they hear the fel-low's gun, be-cause the

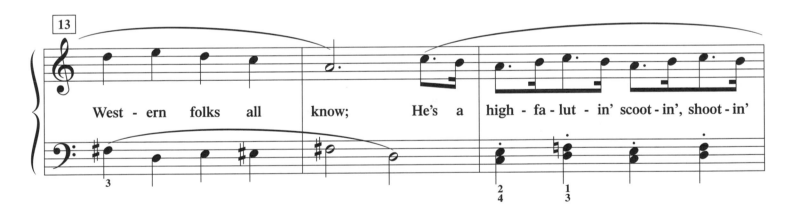

West-ern folks all know; He's a high-fa-lut-in' scoot-in', shoot-in'

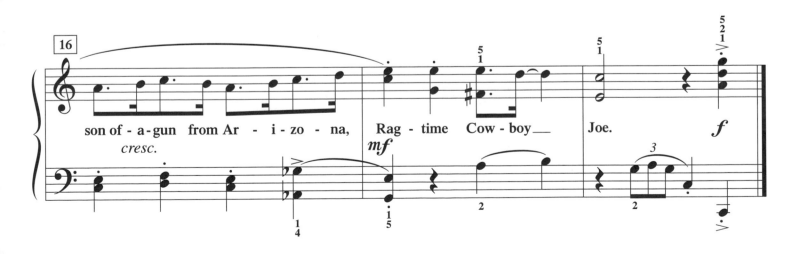

son of-a-gun from Ar-i-zo-na,   Rag-time Cow-boy___ Joe.
cresc.   *mf*   *f*

When Johnny Comes Marching Home

Music and Lyrics by Louis Lambert
arr. Edwin McLean

la - dies, they will all turn out. And we'll all feel gay when

John - ny comes march - ing home.

ABOUT THE PIECES AND COMPOSERS

K-K-K-Katy

Written in 1917 by Geoffrey O'Hara and published the following year, *K-K-K-Katy* tells the story of a love-sick soldier who was too shy to speak to girls. The young man stuttered each time he tried, yet finally found success in declaring his intentions. The original Katy was O'Hara's sister's best friend. Originally from Ontario, Canada, Geoffrey O'Hara taught music at Columbia University and the University of South Dakota, where he composed mainly hymns and other sacred music. None, however, have endured like *K-K-K-Katy*.

My Old Kentucky Home

Published in 1853, Stephen Foster's *My Old Kentucky Home* was adopted as the Kentucky State Song in 1928. The original lyrics made reference to life on a plantation–a reference that the great abolitionist Frederick Douglass felt was very sympathetic to slaves. Still, they were updated after a member of the Kentucky General Assembly filed a complaint in 1986. *My Old Kentucky Home* is sung every year at the start of the Kentucky Derby–known to all as "The Most Exciting Two Minutes in Sports"— and was incorporated into the coin design of the Kentucky state quarter in 2001.

Shine On, Harvest Moon

The moon is a very common subject for popular songs; especially love songs. A search of the song database at the website of ASCAP (the American Society of Composers, Authors and Publishers) reveals over 1,000 songs with the words "moon" or "moonlight" in their title. And this particular "moon" song happens to be the king of them all. First performed in 1908, it is credited to Nora Bayes and Jack Norworth, two of the most popular Broadway performers of that era. But over the years there have been questions about who actually wrote the song. During that time, it was rather common for a songwriter to sell a song outright to a performer who would sometimes add their name to the writing credits. The benefit to such a songwriter was that the song would be performed by an important star, become a hit, and your name would be more recognizable; making it easier to place new songs in the future with publishers and other performers.

About the Pieces and Composers

Maple Leaf Rag

Maple Leaf Rag was one of composer Scott Joplin's earliest works. It was published in 1899, which is three years prior to the publication of Joplin's other signature piece, *The Entertainer*. It reportedly sold over one million copies of sheet music for its first publisher, John Stark & Son of St. Louis, Missouri. The original sheet music cover proudly boasts that Joplin was "King of Ragtime Writers"— a title that he would justify with the publication of *The Entertainer* and the forty-two other rags he composed during his lifetime.

Joplin's rags remained popular with musicians and pianists throughout the years, and enjoyed a tremendous revival in 1973 with the release of the motion picture *The Sting*. This movie's soundtrack was an adaptation of Joplin's music by musician and composer Marvin Hamlisch, and earned the Academy Award for Best Musical Score that year.

Ragtime Cowboy Joe

Originally published back in 1912, this ragtime-style piece became a national hit thanks to a recording by the singer Bob Robert, about which little is known today. The song was used as the theme music for New York City's long running Public Radio show *Cowboy Joe's Radio Ranch*, and has been performed over the years by a diverse group of performers including Alvin and The Chipmunks. Today, the song is used by both the University of Wyoming and the University of California at Davis as their School Fight Song.

When Johnny Comes Marching Home

When Johnny Comes Marching Home is a Civil War-era song that expresses the longing that people have for friends and relatives who are fighting in a war, and how they will celebrate when their loved ones return. The *Johnny* longed for in the song was actually a real person—a Union Army Light Artillery Captain named John O'Rourke—who was away on active duty when the song was written in 1863 by his future brother-in-law Patrick Gilmore (who wrote under the name Louis Lambert).

This song has been adapted in many unique and interesting ways over the years. For example, the noted American composer, Morton Gould, used *Johnny* as the basis for his classical piece *American Salute* and, as recently as 2005, the Irish Rock band U2 performed the tune as part of a medley during their *Vertigo* tour. It was even adapted to become a children's favorite—*The Ants Go Marching One by One*.

ABOUT THE ARRANGERS

Nancy Lau

Nancy Lau (pronounced "Law") has often been told that her music sounds very lyrical and natural. She discovered her love and talent for music early in life. Born with perfect pitch, by age four Nancy was able to play nursery rhymes on the piano by ear. She was soon coming up with her own arrangements of songs and was able to copy any music that she heard.

An active composer, arranger, and piano teacher, Nancy studied music composition with Dr. Norman Weston and piano pedagogy with Nakyong Chai at Saddleback College in Orange County, California. In addition to writing for piano, she has composed for solo voice and chamber ensemble, and has written many choral works. Her compositions have won numerous awards. Nancy maintains a full piano studio, where her emphasis is on keeping music enjoyable and exciting. She believes that students must feel nurtured and accepted, and strives to generate in her piano lessons a joyful experience and positive memory.

Chris Lobdell

Chris Lobdell, a native of Washington State, is nationally established as a composer-arranger, teacher, studio musician, pianist, and producer, whose compositions range from solo piano to full orchestral works. Chris has written and orchestrated for major symphony orchestras, full production shows for various cruise lines, film and video soundtracks for national television commercials, has created MIDI orchestration tracks for several piano series, and has ten years of experience as an MTNA-certified teacher. He continues an 18-year relationship with the music publishing industry as a composer, arranger, and orchestrator, and has over twenty-five books of piano arrangements in worldwide distribution.

In 1988, Chris received the U.S. President's Award for musical arrangements in the nationwide "Take Pride in America" campaign. He has served as a national adjudicator for American Guild of Music (AGM) competitions, and has been a featured presenter of technology workshops at the Florida state affiliate of MTNA and at the AGM national conference. In October of 2003, the Kirkland Orchestra commissioned Mr. Lobdell as orchestrator and featured pianist for the world premier of re-discovered works of Sergei Rachmaninoff, "Sophie's Songs."

Edwin McLean

Edwin McLean is a composer living in Chapel Hill, North Carolina. He is a graduate of the Yale School of Music, where he studied with Krzysztof Penderecki and Jacob Druckman. He also holds a master's degree in music theory and a bachelor's degree in piano performance from the University of Colorado.

Mr. McLean has been the recipient of several grants and awards: The MacDowell Colony, the John Work Award, the Woods Chandler Prize (Yale), Meet the Composer, Florida Arts Council, and many others. He has also won the Aliénor Composition Competition for his work *Sonata for Harpsichord*, published by The FJH Music Company Inc. and recorded by Elaine Funaro (*Into the Millennium*, Gasparo GSCD-331). Since 1979, Edwin McLean has arranged the music of some of today's best known recording artists. Currently, he is senior editor as well as MIDI orchestrator for The FJH Music Company Inc.

ABOUT THE ARRANGERS

Kevin Olson

Kevin Olson is an active pianist, composer, and faculty member at Elmhurst College near Chicago, Illinois, where he teaches classical and jazz piano, music theory, and electronic music. He holds a Doctor of Education degree from National-Louis University, and bachelor's and master's degrees in music composition and theory from Brigham Young University. Before teaching at Elmhurst College, he held a visiting professor position at Humboldt State University in California.

A native of Utah, Kevin began composing at the age of five. When he was twelve, his composition *An American Trainride* received the Overall First Prize at the 1983 National PTA Convention in Albuquerque, New Mexico. Since then, he has been a composer-in-residence at the National Conference on Piano Pedagogy and has written music for the American Piano Quartet, Chicago a cappella, the Rich Matteson Jazz Festival, and several piano teachers associations around the country.

Kevin maintains a large piano studio, teaching students of a variety of ages and abilities. Many of the needs of his own piano students have inspired a diverse collection of books and solos published by The FJH Music Company Inc., which he joined as a writer in 1994.

Robert Schultz

Robert Schultz, composer, arranger, and editor, has achieved international fame during his career in the music publishing industry. The Schultz Piano Library, established in 1980, has included more than 500 publications of classical works, popular arrangements, and Schultz's original compositions in editions for pianists of every level from the beginner through the concert artist. In addition to his extensive library of published piano works, Schultz's output includes original orchestral works, chamber music, works for solo instruments, and vocal music.

Schultz has presented his published editions at workshops, clinics, and convention showcases throughout the United States and Canada. He is a long-standing member of ASCAP and has served as president of the Miami Music Teachers Association. Mr. Schultz's original piano compositions and transcriptions are featured on the compact disc recordings *Visions of Dunbar* and *Tina Faigen Plays Piano Transcriptions*, released on the ACA Digital label and available worldwide. His published original works for concert artists are noted in Maurice Hinson's *Guide to the Pianist's Repertoire, Third Edition*. He currently devotes his full time to composing and arranging. In-depth information about Robert Schultz and The Schultz Piano Library is available at the website www.schultzmusic.com.

USING THE CD

A great way to prepare for your recitals is to listen to the CD.

Enjoy listening to these wonderful pieces anywhere anytime! Listen to them casually (as background music) and attentively. After you have listened to the CD you might discuss interpretation with your teacher and follow along with your score as you listen.

LISTENING ACTIVITY

Listen to the CD and circle the BEST answer:

1. **Which piece has an *ostinato* pattern in the left hand?**

   The Rock Island Line (Track 1)

   My Old Kentucky Home (Track 8)

2. **Which piece is in $\frac{3}{4}$ time?**

   In the Good Old Summer Time (Track 2)

   K-K-K-Katy (Track 7)

3. **Which piece is bright and energetic?**

   The Yankee Doodle Boy (Track 3)

   The House of the Rising Sun (Track 6)

4. **Which piece has grace notes that sound like bagpipes in Scotland?**

   The Campbells Are Comin' (Track 4)

   The Glow-Worm (Track 5)

5. **Which piece has several triplets in it?**

   K-K-K-Katy (Track 7)

   Shine On, Harvest Moon (Track 9)

6. **Which piece is an example of syncopation?**

   Maple Leaf Rag (Track 10)

   When Johnny Comes Marching Home (Track 12)

Which piece(s) is/are your FAVORITE?

_____

_____

_____

_____

_____

Answers: 1. The Rock Island Line 2. In the Good Old Summer Time 3. The Yankee Doodle Boy 4. The Campbells Are Comin' 5. K-K-K-Katy 6. Maple Leaf Rag